Get Lifted
With PDMK Daily Devotionals

PROPHET DARRELL M. KEITH

WESTBOW
PRESS®
A DIVISION OF THOMAS NELSON
& ZONDERVAN

Copyright © 2022 Prophet Darrell M. Keith.

All rights reserved. No part of this book may be used or reproduced by any means, graphic, electronic, or mechanical, including photocopying, recording, taping or by any information storage retrieval system without the written permission of the author except in the case of brief quotations embodied in critical articles and reviews.

This book is a work of non-fiction. Unless otherwise noted, the author and the publisher make no explicit guarantees as to the accuracy of the information contained in this book and in some cases, names of people and places have been altered to protect their privacy.

WestBow Press books may be ordered through booksellers or by contacting:

WestBow Press
A Division of Thomas Nelson & Zondervan
1663 Liberty Drive
Bloomington, IN 47403
www.westbowpress.com
844-714-3454

Because of the dynamic nature of the Internet, any web addresses or links contained in this book may have changed since publication and may no longer be valid. The views expressed in this work are solely those of the author and do not necessarily reflect the views of the publisher, and the publisher hereby disclaims any responsibility for them.

Any people depicted in stock imagery provided by Getty Images are models, and such images are being used for illustrative purposes only. Certain stock imagery © Getty Images.

Scripture taken from the King James Version of the Bible.

Scripture quotations taken from The Holy Bible, New International Version® NIV® Copyright © 1973 1978 1984 2011 by Biblica, Inc. TM. Used by permission. All rights reserved worldwide.

Scripture taken from the Amplified Bible, Copyright © 1954, 1958, 1962, 1964, 1965, 1987 by The Lockman Foundation. Used with permission.

Scripture quotations marked (NLT) are taken from the Holy Bible, New Living Translation, copyright ©1996, 2004, 2015 by Tyndale House Foundation. Used by permission of Tyndale House Publishers, a Division of Tyndale House Ministries, Carol Stream, Illinois 60188. All rights reserved.

"Scripture quotations are from the ESV® Bible (The Holy Bible, English Standard Version®), copyright © 2001 by Crossway, a publishing ministry of Good News Publishers. Used by permission. All rights reserved."

"New Revised Standard Version Bible, copyright 1989, Division of Christian Education of the National Council of the Churches of Christ in the United States of America. Used by permission. All rights reserved."

Scripture taken from the New King James Version® Copyright © 1982 by Thomas Nelson. Used by permission. All rights reserved.

Scripture taken from the Holy Bible: International Standard Version®. Copyright © 1996-forever by The ISV Foundation. ALL RIGHTS RESERVED INTERNATIONALLY. Used by permission.

Scripture quotations marked (GNT) are from the Good News Translation in Today's English Version- Second Edition Copyright © 1992 by American Bible Society. Used by Permission.

Scripture taken from the Contemporary English Version © 1991, 1992, 1995 by American Bible Society. Used by Permission.

ISBN: 978-1-6642-8317-6 (sc)
ISBN: 978-1-6642-8318-3 (hc)
ISBN: 978-1-6642-8319-0 (e)

Library of Congress Control Number: 2022920639

Print information available on the last page.

WestBow Press rev. date: 01/23/2023

DAY 1

Today, God dropped the word (PUSH) in my spirit. When I looked up the word: it means to move forward by using force to pass people or cause them to move aside.

YOUR HOUR OF THE PUSH IS HERE!

You've been commissioned by the Holy Ghost to yield your members. It's time to push with every facet of your being. God has a court side seat watching every step during your next game. Your mind is different. You are a lethal weapon in God's Kingdom and demons, imps, devil, snakes, and every creature from beneath the sub-terrestrial world will be defeated! Get up as we take dominion! Where's your sword and helmet? It's time to suit up!

Today's assignment is as follows:

You must pray three times today and declare twelve things that I need to be shaken right now. I feel cloven tongues of fire! Go ahead, he is waiting….

God that is it!

Stay blessed, because you are blessed!

Amen

DAY 2

Your mind is a weapon!

Your shout delivers champions, and your voice causes devils to fall. Your tongue will scatter serpents and everything you decree will come to pass! It's another day that the Lord has made, and I feel like decreeing! I have been set up by God to take my place and so have you all! Today, we know according to scholars that he has risen, but one thing I also know that He rose in me! Get up with your anointed self and snatch your family, money, and power back from that liar (Satan) of course! I'm counting on you guys!

Amen

DAY 3

Did you know that hump day (which is Wednesday) gets its name because of Judas? It was Wednesday before the crucifixion that Judas conspired to hand Jesus over. For this he was paid thirty pieces of silver (Mt. 26:14 KJV). The thing about that was he died before he spent it. I'm convinced that God got our backs because of what He suffered just for us. That's why we are going to serve God with all our might. Get Ready! I feel contractions from the spiritual baby I'm about to give birth to! You owe God the praise! The hour is here where every demon that tried to kill you won't live to tell it. Suit up, take your position, and push like never before!

Amen

DAY 4

Did you know that on June 10, 1952, Benjamin Franklin took a kite through a thunderstorm to prove that lightning and electricity were both the same? After reading this I told God let this be the day that all of us get electrified. I pray that an energy will hit your body that the devil himself can't stop! I feel the Holy Ghost with a burning fire. Saints the Word says that what we bind on earth will be bound in heaven and I just bound the enemy. We will win and he will lose! My spiritual weapons are authoritative and so are yours......5, 4, 3, 2, 1!

You are on! Let's go, in Jesus' name!

Amen

DAY 5

Saints of the Most High, as I was laying here earlier; The Lord began to download a few things in my spirit. He said that the world will get worse, but the saints shall birth wealth. Those that don't have Christ won't survive the shaken but those that have Him shall triumph in victory. Your houses will thrive and lack will be your enemy. Sound the alarms and stay on your faces, as the season approaches. Pray for our families and nation, that the people can turn to the voice of God, so He can heal the land.

Amen

DAY 6

Jesus is more than just the written and the spoken word; He is "The Message".

Today I am making a decree that men and women of every different kind of origin will hearken to the voice of the almighty God. Did you know that it was only once a year in the biblical times that people were allowed to bring their problems to the temple? We can come to God whenever we like. I command that your prayer life shifts 7 times greater. Every word you utter to God will come to pass, in Jesus's name!

Amen

DAY 7

The Lord just spoke to me as I worshiped and said: "We that remain in my presence for the Kingdom of Satan must come down. Know that my Covenant will not be broken for those that carry my blood." Whatever you do; don't let the enemy steal your joy because familiar spirits are real and even in dreams, they can be deposited. Let us move forward to the light and cast Satan out, for good! I prophesied that there will be a coin shortage and it's happening all over the globe. People are storing coins as I speak. The Gospel says: "The kingdom of God suffered violence and the violent taketh by force" (Matthew 11:12 NKJV). It's time to take your place like never before! Put on your entire armor as we launch our gifts and stir up the calling of God, out of the depths of our guts!

Whew!

That gave me chills!

Amen

DAY 8

I am on an all-time high!

When God moves, He moves! Saints have been calling and confirming the great news of their prophecies coming to pass! God never ceases to amaze me.

Today's scripture is as follows: (Isaiah 40:31 NIV) But those who hope in the Lord will renew their strength. They will soar on wings like eagles; they will run and not grow weary; they will walk and not be faint. Lace and tie your shoes because this race is just now getting started! Suit up and we are days away from something new and life changing! Glory!

Amen

DAY 9

The number 25 means "Grace upon Grace". Grace is happening now because of the people who are praying. As the world evolves, the people of God are becoming revolutionary (involving drastic change). We will follow Christ with every facet of our being! Jesus, knowing his disciples are struggling in the middle of Galilee, begins to walk on water toward the ship. Around 3am (Mark 6:48 AMP) the disciples, at a distance of 25 to 30 furlongs (3:1-3.7 miles or 5-6 kilometers) from where they left, seeing Christ walking toward them. The moment the Lord gets in the ship it is miraculously transported to their destination (John 6:21 KJV). Miracles are back!

Amen

DAY 10

The revelation about the dirt blew my mind! For example, can you imagine someone trying to bury you with word curses, hatred, and jealousy. Then later they found out you were a seed, and you grew right up out of the very trap that was set for you! Greetings to you all from our King and Savior! He is everything! Our scripture is as follows: (2Peter 1:3 ESV) His divine power has granted to us all things that pertain to life and godliness, through the knowledge of him who called us to his own glory and excellence. Do not let anyone steal your joy. What you have in you must be added to and not taken away from. You all are awesome!

Amen

DAY 11

The New Testament tells us about the days before Christ's return will be like the days of Noah (Matthew 24:37; Luke 17:36 NKJV). The reason God told Noah he was sending the flood was: for the earth is filled with violence" (Genesis 6:13 NKJV). In 2018 there were 16,214 reported murderers in the United States; that is 44 a day; 1.8 every hour. Violence fills the earth. It's prayer time and proof that we are on one accord with the spirit. It's time to trust God more than ever. At this point our country is clearly in trouble. Peace, love, joy, unity, and equality are the things that make any environment prosper and thrive. I'm praying that God will inherit the praise of His people. Stay suited! Our world needs it! I'm so ready for everything God has for his people! Our praise is a weapon and it's been time to use it.

Amen

DAY 12

This morning I had a vision of a woman singing on stage and then she fell dead. Suddenly, she got up and said: "I heard the trumpet of the Lord sound and I awakened." The people were running wild, and she said that the Lord brought me back to tell you all that "HE IS REAL AND HIS RETURN IS REAL "She started telling people to get their souls right because the hour has come! She was dressed in a blue dress and high heels but after she died, she got up. Her whole countenance was changed as she spoke. The glory of the Lord filled the house.

Amen

DAY 13

Woke up to an early start glorifying God and the beauty of holiness to the 5th power! (Ephesians 6:12 KJV) For we wrestle not against flesh and blood, but against principalities, against powers, against rulers of the darkness of this world, against spiritual wickedness in high places. Wow! Knowing that we are tearing down spiritual wickedness in high places, is a relief knowing that strongholds will finally be broken off people's lives. I live for this. Serving God is like basketball. Although your problems may spin around your finger, remember it's you that is controlling it. You have the power to stop anything that keeps you from scoring. I prophesy today: that strongholds are shattered, and chains dissipated! Your Monday is fiery, lit, powerful, Dunamis, upbeat, supernatural, joyous, and contagious! Every demon must stand down because you win.

Amen

DAY 14

Word for today: God will fight for you! When Hezekiah was king of Judah, the powerful nation of Assyria marched into their land and threatened Jerusalem. The commander of the Assyrians taunted the Judean king, even offering to give him 2,000 horses for their upcoming battle (2 Kings 18:23 KJV). Hezekiah went into the temple and prayed for God to intervene. That night, the angel of the Lord decimated the Assyrian army, forcing them to head back to their own country (2 Kings 19:35-36 KJV). The enemy has and will always be defeated! Stay suited and assume the position!

Amen

DAY 15

There are thousands upon thousands who are willing to gain the whole world and lose their souls (Mark 8:36 KJV). I want wealth but not at the expense of my soul. That's why through Jesus, we can have them both. The bible tells us above all things prosper and be in good health: even as your soul prosper (3 John 1:2 KJV). In God we can have so much power, wealth, health, and authority, that we can share with all that are in need. (Mark 10:45) For even the son of man did not come to be served, but to serve, and to give his life as a ransom for many. We thank you Lord that even now your promise from Revelation is true: "I am making everything new!" (Rev. 21:5 KJV) Through this I'm healthy, wealthy, and victorious!

Amen

DAY 16

Today, not only do I realize that I'm professing Christianity, but I have a desire to be more like Christ! The Dichotomy of "The World Verses the Heavens" is nothing to even think about debating. We are intended to be delegates of the heavens and knowing that the earth will never be eternal. My mind is made up and my impact will inspire more to be like Christ. The whole objective is to free yourself from sin and help many others to vanquish their sin nature. Wow! (I'm running in the spirit!) Our relationship with God impacts our entire life. Faith in Christ should not only determine how we spend our Sunday mornings but also how we live our lives for the rest of the week. We cannot allow the truth that Jesus died for our sin to become justification for sinning (Rom. 6:1–2 KJV). Our prayers and worship are not limited to Sunday. We are to be consistent and faithful in our walk with Christ every day. Thank you, God, for your grace and for the sustaining power of the Holy Spirit.

Amen

DAY 17

We understand that we all have sinned and come short of His glory (Romans 3:23 KJV). But when God free us from bondage; It's our goal to stay liberated. Who the Son sets free is free indeed! David realized what he done was totally wrong. He begins his prayer by pleading to God for mercy, "Have mercy on me, O God" (Ps. 51:1-7 KJV). He knows that he does not deserve God's forgiveness.

His hope is in the compassion of God (v. 1). David clearly and honestly acknowledges his sin. He realizes that his sin comes from a deep place within him, "Surely, I was sinful at birth, sinful from the time my mother conceived me" (v. 5). He prays for God not only to forgive him but also to cleanse him and restore him to a state of holiness (v. 7). God doesn't restore anything back to its original state but always make it better than before. (John 8:36 KJV) "If the Son therefore shall make you free, ye shall be free indeed." Finally, David declares that in his restored state, he will engage in ministry. He will "teach" transgressors God's ways so that sinners will turn back to Him. He desires to use his new life to declare God's praise. So, Embrace Your Freedom, Embrace Your Fire, Embrace Your Power, Let Go and Let God! I'm Running! For surely the time is now!

Amen

DAY 18

It's time to sharpen our skills and know that God is God! In today's reading of the Word David declares, "The fool says in his heart, 'There is no God'" (Psalms 53:1 KJV) David is not referring to a philosophical atheist—that kind of person did not likely exist in the ancient world. Rather, this "fool" is a functional atheist—a person who lives as if God does not see or care. There are consequences to this kind of unbelief. The lack of a moral standard or sense of accountability leads to corrupt and destructive actions. (ROMANS 3:23 KJV) For all have sinned and fallen short of the glory of God. Well today, we are choosing to free ourselves from every entanglement orchestrated by Satan himself. Suit up and take your positions as we glorify God today!

Amen

DAY 19

When David needed guidance, he always went to God. When he was rebellious, he still knew that not obeying God was the reason why things were complicated. David's nephew Abishai offered to pin Saul to the ground with one thrust of a spear, arguing that God had delivered the king into David's hands. Once more, David chose to leave matters in God's hands. He explained to Abishai, "The Lord forbid that I should lay a hand on the Lord's anointed" (1 Samuel 24:11 KJV). David Said: "When I am afraid, I put my trust in you. In God, whose word I praise in God, I trust and am not afraid." (Psalm 56:3–4 KJV) Like David, we receive guidance from God in three major ways. First, God provides clear direction through His Word. Second, He guides us through wise counsel from others. Third, He often confirms his direction through circumstances. Give everything to God and just leave it and watch God move. I'm running now because in God, nothing can go wrong. It takes the wrong things to make everything right. Suit up and move out into the deep things of God!

Amen

DAY 20

You are not alone. God wants me to let you all know that He is there watching and listening to every word you utter. The angels are waiting to fight at your command. If you've ever lost a loved one, friend, parent or a spouse, may these words from (Psalm 68:5) comfort you: "A father to the fatherless, a defender of widows, is God in his holy dwelling" you are not alone. Praise His Holy Name! Psalm 68 celebrates both God's transcendent power and his fatherly care for each person. Thank the Lord today that both aspects of God are true. We can also look forward to the day when we will experience God's presence in person (Rev. 21:3 KJV). Ecclesiastes!! GOD was then, now, and will always be! Stay on beast mode and know that God has given you power to tread over serpents and scorpions! You are indeed victorious!

Amen

DAY 21

You will not walk in fear. Everything the devil meant for evil has been turned around for your good. Your mind is a weapon, sound and resolute. You are fearless and powerful. The fruit of your labor are in a season of manifestation. Get ready and prepare for the increase! Moses experienced fear. When God called him to deliver Israel from Egypt, Moses was afraid that his own people would not listen to him, that Pharaoh would not respect him, and that he could not speak well enough to accomplish the job (Exodus 13–14 NKJV). Even so, God worked through Moses. His fear was overcome by God's promise to be with him every step of the way. God made you all a promise and it will surely come to pass! Your steps have been ordained and anointed to finish this year and prepare for the greater that's coming! It shall be done! In The Mighty Name of Jesus!

Amen

DAY 22

As we get closer to the coming of our Lord; the people of God are losing their focus and their fire, but God also warned us of this. We that are burning for God's passion have the power to bring hope to those that are lost! It's time to mature in the gospel and know that - not only is it important for us to be saved but our loved ones as well. I'm not afraid of Satan and his works because he is POWERLESS TO THE BELIEVERS!! I'm Shouting! (1 Samuel 22 KJV) David was hiding in a cave, but he knew his real refuge was God alone. May we as believers find our security, protection, and confidence in the Lord, and not in the things of this world. (Mark 16:15 KJV) "And he said unto them, go ye into all the world, and preach the gospel to every creature." In a world where each nation worshiped their own deities, David affirmed that the God of Israel is the God over all nations and people. His glory is over all the earth!

Amen

DAY 23

Today's hour requires us to pray without cease against every attack and every trick that will dilute the plans of the enemy! We will pray and defeat him in our lives. VICTORY BELONGS TO JESUS! David asks God to "break the teeth of the enemies' mouths: "O God! LORD, tear out the fangs of those lions!" (Psalms 58:6 KJV). David prays that these rulers would become powerless to continue their oppression. David is honest with God about his desire for their defeat. (Psalms 58:7-10 KJV) David's ultimate desire was for justice to be done, so that people will know that "there is a God who judges the earth" (Psalms 58:11 KJV). Today, we pray for believers around the world who are suffering for their faith. They endure injustice and persecution, but you, the Lord of justice, the righteous Judge is on their side. We praise You—Your truth will prevail!

Amen

DAY 24

No Matter What You Face in Life, Trust God in Everything!

Whatever the enemy tries to block in God is the proof that it belongs to you. It is easy to say, "I trust in God," when things are going well. However, when a crisis hits, our trust is put to the test. True contentment and security are a gift that comes from God alone. "Truly my soul finds rest in God: my salvation comes from him" (Psalms 62:1 KJV). For God is our refuge. He is the only source of true power. David knows that his temporary failure doesn't mean that God's promises have failed. He trusts that God will be able to make things right. Psalm 60(KJV) provides us with a model of how to relate to God in times when His promises seem unfulfilled. We can be honest with God and claim His promises. We can remind ourselves that we do not fully understand what God is doing, but we are going to trust him anyway. Never let go of God's promises because they shall surely come to pass!

Amen

DAY 25

I know beyond a shadow of doubt; we were created to serve God and Him alone! The more this world gets corrupt, I find myself like David: (PSALM 63:1 NIV) "I thirst for you, my whole being longs for you in a dry and parched land where there is no water". As a dry and cracked desert landscape needs water for life to flourish, David knows that he needs intimacy with God in order to survive. In the early church a man named Father Augustine said: "that his soul was empty until he found God. When he found God; He began to thank him both day and night. He told God these words: "You made us for yourself, and our hearts are restless until they find rest in you." I'm thirsty for God, saints; no matter what happens in this world, we owe God the praise!

We were born for this!

Amen

DAY 26

Today is a great day to shabach our Lord! He is definitely worthy!

What is the difference between the righteous and the wicked? Is it simply, that the righteous generally do the right thing while the wicked do not? David's hope in a just God is our hope as well. While in this life the wicked may seem to get away with evil, we know that ultimately justice will be done. "The fear of the LORD is the beginning of knowledge, but fools despise wisdom and instruction" (PROVERBS 1:7 NIV). No matter what happens in this life always strive to be righteous and to do the right things in this world. We are held to a higher standard and righteousness always prevails. Like a boomerang, the attacks of the enemy will bounce off you and rebound upon themselves. God's justice will lead people to both proclaim the glory of God as well as giving him praise!

Amen

DAY 27

As we know fasting is a sacrificial offering from the things that sustain our flesh! Daniel told the enemy regardless of whatever you eat, I will still have more energy (power) than any of you. Daniel, who limited his diet to vegetables and water to be able to cleanse his body and better focus on a spiritual connection to God, left behind every distraction to win against the wiles of the devil. "In those days I, Daniel, was mourning three full weeks. I ate no pleasant food, no meat or anything wrong came into my mouth, nor did I anoint myself at all, till three whole weeks were fulfilled." (Daniel 10:2-3 KJV). I'm after something powerful! Saints the time is now! I'm running! I feel like Esther! "Go, gather all the Jews to be found in Susa, and hold a fast on my behalf, and do not eat or drink for three days, night or day. I and my young women will also fast as you do. Then I will go to the king, though it is against the law, and if I perish, I perish" (Esther 4:16 ISV).

Amen

DAY 28

My ultimate goal in this walk of life is to see God face to face! In order to do that I must continue to tear down the walls and barriers which stagnates our daily move consistently! Just like the caterpillar, when our process is complete, what we change into is worth the cocoon. "Our God is a God who saves "(PSALM 68:20 GNT). It is important to recognize that God uses His power to help and protect the most vulnerable in society. He will give you the power you need to fight against the wiles of the devil. You are undefeated at any rate. Psalm 68 celebrates both God's transcendent power and His fatherly care for each person. Thank the Lord today that both aspects of God are true. We can also look forward to the day when we will experience God's presence in person (Rev. 21:3 KJV).

Amen

DAY 29

Truly God has lit a fire down in my soul! Out of the mist of it all, my heart speaks! Truly deliverance and love for God could never be hid, as hatred, drugs, sex, etc.... increases, my love for God and the saving of souls grows stronger. Regardless of the hand that life dwelt you in the beginning; doesn't have to be that hand in the end. David recognized that he could not solve his problems by himself. He needed God's help, and he needed it quickly. In the gospels, a father asked Jesus to heal his son (Psalm 70 NIV). Jesus said if you really believe, I could do it! The father replied, "I do believe; help me overcome my unbelief" (Mark 9:24 NIV). I challenge you today to believe in the power of who God is and the ability that he placed in you. You are more than just a conqueror. You are God's chosen delegate officials and today I weaponize you. Take your positions and never get weary in well doing.

Amen

DAY 30

Grab Your Word and Catch It Like a Fisherman at Bayside! You are sharpened and equipped to handle this day and many more great ones that lie ahead. Jesus Christ not only gives God's Word to us humans; He is the Word. The logos is God, begotten and therefore distinguishable from the Father, but being God, of the same substance (essence). "For I am convinced that neither death nor life, neither angels nor demons, neither the present nor the future, nor any powers, neither height nor depth, nor anything else in all creation, will be able to separate us from the love of God that is in Christ Jesus our Lord "(Romans 8:38-39 NIV). God Is Saying: "I have loved you with an everlasting love" (Jeremiah 31:3KJV).

"I formed you in your mother's (Jeremiah 1:5 NLT) womb." "If you seek my face, you will find me." (2 Chronicles 15:2 KJV) Stay Strong and Prepare for The Best Days of Your Mortal Lives!

Amen

DAY 31

I'm praying that you and your loved ones remained safe after Tropical Storm Zeta left her mark upon the land! It's often when we go through "Storms of Life" and God yet delivers only to make it better. There are three types of storms we deal with in life: Perfecting Storms, Protecting Storms, and Correcting Storms. There's no place you can go where the Lord is not there. To me it's reassuring to know that wherever I go or whatever I face in life, God is with me! And the good news about storms is they have a beginning, a middle and an end. Maybe your storm has been raging for a while. But you know what? You might be at the end of it. So don't give up. God rescued Jonah from the belly of a fish, so you know God can get you out of whatever you're facing right now.

Amen

DAY 32

There are tons of people without power including some of us! We had to throw out food and declare strength so that the enemy wouldn't attack our faith. We will not be moved! Today we declare a miracle! A miracle is a phenomenon not explained by known laws of nature. Miracles showed the compassion Jesus had for people. This can be seen when Jesus healed the paralyzed man because of the faith of his friends. This teaches us to have faith. Miracles demonstrated the close relationship Jesus had with God, His Father. Please continue to pray for our country, our people, and our nations as we continue to tear down strongholds in our region!

Today We Declare Miracles Starting with Us!

Amen

DAY 33

In time pass, it was awkward not having church services. That's why it's very important to have God in and on your heart for such a time like this! Whatever you do, don't allow the enemy to steal your peace. The devil is loose and not just in our economy. Jesus promised that the coming of the Spirit would empower the disciples to tell others about Him (Acts 1:8 KJV). The effect upon Peter was evident as he stood boldly and explained that what these visitors were seeing had been predicted by the Prophet Joel. Peter preached the gospel, emphasized the resurrection, and called them to turn to Christ. "Repent and be baptized, every one of you, in the name of Jesus Christ for the forgiveness of sins" (Acts 2:38NIV). He promised that all who did so would also receive the gift of the Holy Spirit. Be careful how we witness. Because we want to bring souls to Christ. Don't drive them away! Help me bring God's Kingdom to all that thirst.

Amen

DAY 34

As you know it's debate time and I'm praying for earth. The Bible declares, "And from the days of John the Baptist until now the kingdom of heaven suffered violence, and the violent took it by force "(Matthew 11:12 KJV). We have been commissioned by the Holy Spirit to take dominion and bring the ways of God to all that know Him! It takes realness, unity, and God to all who will let Him! I'm running because the evil one is always at work; our vigilance cannot be relaxed —not even for a moment. A small and seemingly innocent invitation can turn into a tall temptation which can lead to tragic transgression. Night and day, at home or away, we must shun sin and "Hold fast, which is good."
(1 Thessalonians 5:21)

These priceless blessings can be ours if we set our houses in order now and faithfully cling to the gospel.

God lives! Jesus is the Christ! This is His Church!

Amen

DAY 35

Did you all know that just like the Trinity we existed but just not made yet! Before I formed thee in the belly, I knew thee; and before thou came forth out of the womb, I sanctified thee, and I ordained thee a prophet unto the nations "(Jeremiah 1:5 KJV). Abraham is someone mentioned in Genesis, thousands of years before Jesus came to earth. Yet, Jesus said of himself, "Before Abraham was born, I am" (John 8:58-59 KJV). The Jews understood fully what Jesus was saying because they picked up stones to kill him for "blasphemy" - claiming to be God. Jesus has always existed. God knows your outcome and the plans he has for your lives! Plans to prosper you and not harm you! Plans to give you an expected end! Have an awesome blessed day men and women of God and know that God will always be your God!

Whew!

I'm running, because He is so good!

Be encouraged!

Amen

DAY 36

In Acts 12, the church experienced two surprises that demonstrated God's intervention and provision. The first was Peter's deliverance from prison, which even had elements of humor. While the church prayed, Peter was asleep, seeming untroubled by his predicament. In fact, he slept so soundly that the angel struck him on the side to wake him up! The second was Peter's surprise arrival at their prayer meeting. Despite their earnest prayers, the church was stunned when Peter showed up at the door. By the time you finish praying today; We are declaring that divine shifts will spring up around you and everything you love. You are expecting and anticipating God's mighty work which will be done in your lives. Do not be afraid. Your Heavenly Father knows what you need even before you ask (Matt. 6:8 KJV).

Amen

DAY 37

Just to remind you of how much power you have: No weapon that is formed against you will succeed, and every tongue that rises against you in judgment you will condemn. This [peace, righteousness, security and triumph over opposition] is the heritage of the servants of the Lord, and this is their vindication from Me, says the Lord (Isaiah 54:17 AMP). The LORD will make you the head, not the tail. If you pay attention to the commands of the LORD your God that I give you this day and carefully follow them, you will always be at the top, never at the bottom. (Deuteronomy 28:13 AMP). And this same God who takes care of me will supply all your needs from his glorious riches, which have been given to us in Christ Jesus (Philippians 4:19 NLT). Just wanted to charge you for battle. Suit up because this race has to be for the ones that endure to the end.

I'm Running!

Amen

DAY 38

Most people know the name of Jesus, but they may not understand fully who he is? They have important gaps in their understanding. After a year in Corinth, Paul set out again, dropping off Priscilla and Aquila at Ephesus. There they met Apollos, who taught what he already knew about Jesus accurately enough but "knew only the baptism of John" (Acts 18:25 KJV). The couple filled in the gaps in Apollo's information, and he went on to be powerful defender of the gospel. Meanwhile, Paul arrived in Ephesus, where he met other former disciples of John. They also needed more information about Jesus. They had been baptized by John but not "in the name of the Lord Jesus" (Acts 19:5 KJV). When we understand fully who He is; signs and wonders follow including fire. The Sons of Sceva tried to cast out demons and the demons spoke back saying: "Jesus, I know, and Paul I know about, but who are you" (Acts 19:15 KJV)? We praise you, Lord, as a powerful Creator, the source of truth and grace, and the giver of true freedom. Give us courage and discernment to follow you wholeheartedly, with commitment and strong faith.

Amen

DAY 39

Time to rise with power and kick the week off to a great start. Let God continue to move in your life because your good work will payoff soon. Don't let nothing stop you from thriving. It's your mission to evolve. Bringing change to all who know the God that we serve. In Genesis 6, God is very sad and disappointed about the wickedness that has overtaken humanity. Reluctantly, he decides to wipe out the human race and start from scratch. Noah, however, is the only one who has been good. The story is very powerful. God tells him to build an ark that will save him, his family, and animal life. As he is boarding the ark, God says to him, "for you alone I have seen to be righteous before Me in this time" (Genesis 7:1 NIV). Literally the whole world was doing what was wrong. But did that stop Noah from doing what was right? Not a chance! Whew! Always do what's right; even when you are alone. Because God knows your heart and He alone wants to perfect us. Through our weakness we are made strong. Let's start out with an eviction notice to Satan! Glory!

Amen

DAY 40

Just a quick parable that hit my spirit. An elementary school teacher told her class to be ready because in the coming week there will be a fire alarm. She taught them what they should do when the bell rang. They would need to follow directions and act promptly. But, of course, she didn't tell them when. They were to be ready to respond because the alarm could ring at any moment!

Matthew 24:36-44 King James Version 36 But of that day and hour knoweth no man, no, not the angels of heaven, but my Father only. 37 But as the days of Noah were, so shall also the coming of the Son of man be. 38 For as in the days that were before the flood they were eating and drinking, marrying and giving in marriage, until the day that Noe entered the ark, 39 And knew not until the flood came, and took them all away; so, shall also the coming of the Son of man be. 40 Then shall two be in the field; the one shall be taken, and the other left. 41 Two women shall be grinding at the mill; the one shall be taken, and the other left. 42 Watch therefore: for ye know not what hour your Lord doth come. 43 But know this, that if the goodman of the house had known what watch the thief would come, he would have watched, and would not have suffered his house to be broken up. 44 Therefore be ye also ready: for in such an hour as ye think not the son of man cometh.

You can protect your future by yielding to the Spirit's control and pursuing what scripture considers most valuable: knowing, loving, obeying, and serving God. This investment reaps long-term blessings that continue into eternity.

Amen

DAY 41

Just want to give a little food for thought! Hope your day will be blessed immensely!

Here's Today's Word:

Many people mistakenly believe that when Jesus said "Do not judge" in Matthew 7:1 KJV, He meant that we should never make a judgment about another's behavior. They ignore the fact that Jesus also told his disciples not to "give dogs what is sacred" or "throw your pearls to pigs," two commands which require an assessment of character (Matt. 7:6 KJV). Jesus' command not to judge is a warning about the danger of judging others without first judging yourself (Matt. 7:3–5 KJV). His main point is that we should apply the same standard to ourselves that we use for others. We must look in the mirror first at ourselves and make sure we are in place before we help by pointing fingers at others. Life is too short to remain unrefined. Have an amazing day folks!

Amen

DAY 42

I pray the devotion brings a sense of comfort your way.

The Bible says that when we are sick or going through life's difficulties; we can come boldly to the throne of God, asking for grace and mercy in our time of need. Though our bodies don't feel well, or depression tries to creep in, God still rules over our circumstances and Jesus still have the power and authority to heal us, not to mention His willingness and ability to do so. Approach Jesus with faith and expectancy, believing that He still heals the sick, removes all depression, sets us free, and exercises dominion over our physical bodies. We will all go through sometimes, but that doesn't mean that Jesus isn't interested in healing your body, mind, and soul today. Confidently call out to Him to bring healing into your life. Prayer: Jesus, I thank you that you have both the power and authority to heal my broken spirit! I boldly come to you today to ask for your grace and healing power to be at work in my soul! I trust that you are powerful and looking for an opportunity to show your power in my life! Cause this sickness and broken spirit to leave my body in Jesus' name. I break the power of stress and trauma and release your peace. I speak to every part of my body and say, "Be whole in Jesus' name." Function properly—the way God designed you to function. Jesus, send your word and heal me today. You paid the price for my healing, so I trust that you are at work with me. Holy Spirit, fill every part of me with your supernatural presence. Drive out all that is not good, holy, and true. I receive the healing you have for me today, in Jesus' name.

Amen

DAY 43

Today we are preparing for a newness in God. We will tear down every wall that may have alienated you from the promises or divine presence of God. Well, get ready! As we prepare for the takeover demonstrating in oil, fire, and power, the works of the devil are being destroyed! God not only promised the physical restoration of His people, but He also promised that they would become what they always were meant to be: a haven for those who seek the Lord and want to live in the right relationship with Him. We declare and decree that during this season of tranquility: that the blessings of "The Lord "overtake us! Every blessing we enjoy comes from God. He chose us. He "predestined us for adoption to sonship" (Ephesians 1:5 NIV). He redeemed us. He lavished us with grace. He revealed to us the "mystery of his will". He has given us the Holy Spirit. All these benefits and more have come to us because of the person and work of Jesus Christ. These blessings were given to us not simply for our enjoyment, but so that we would be equipped to take part in God's mission to the world while we look forward to our eternal inheritance. We shall and will do our very best as we take down Satan and his army one demon at a time! Prepare for battle!

Amen

DAY 44

Just a little morning inspiration to jumpstart your day!

"Trust in the LORD with all your heart and lean not on your own understanding. in all your ways acknowledge Him, and He shall direct your paths" (PROVERBS 3:5-6 NKJV)

Lord, I come to you today with an open heart and mind, trusting you to lead me. My "go-to" move is to try to work things out in my own standing, but that often leads to worry and exhaustion. I know that your ways are higher than my ways and that you see the bigger picture. Today, I'm letting go of my need to control how things turn out. I lean into your love and trust that you know what you're doing much better than I do. Help me to remember that you are a good Father, always directing me with gentleness and wisdom!

Amen

DAY 45

Positive Influence

"Let your light shine before men in such à way that they may see your good works and glorify your Father who is in heaven" (MATTHEW 5:16 KJV). Lord, I know that you have given me everything I need to live a life like yours. As I love others with mercy, may they realize how incredibly merciful you are. As I live with a heart of compassion toward all, may others catch on to how compassionate you are. When I treat others with kindness, no matter their station or attitude, may it reflect your own inclusive kindness. Let all I do line up with your character. When it doesn't, let me be quick to repent and seek forgiveness and reconciliation, revealing your magnanimous heart that is swift to forgive. Be glorified in my life, no matter what happens in this world; let your light shine so bright that no one could ever kill or assassinate your joy!

Amen

DAY 46

As we look in the mirror, we hope to iron out wrinkles and be more presentable before God so that He can use us to bring others to the fold. "If anyone is in Christ, there is a new creation: everything old has passed away, see, everything has become new" 2 CORINTHIANS 5:17 NRSV! I need your love to drive out the anxieties that build in the pressure cooker of my nervous system. God, you are everything I need. Don't turn your back when I cry out to you. I know you won't. You don't grow weary of kindly reassuring your children when they start to squirm at the unfamiliar. It is we that grow weary. You are my help and my hope. And today, I take a stand to fight the enemy at thy very gate. Jeremiah 29:11 KJV, tells me that you've planned to give me hope and a future with an expected ending.

Amen

DAY 47

I woke up this morning thanking God for my commitment. It's important that we walk in love with a readiness upon the arrival of that great day. Fully committed, "Devote yourselves completely to the LORD our God, walking in his statutes and keeping his commandments, as on this day" (1 KINGS 8:61 NRSV). Thank you, God, that as I keep coming back to you, I am reminded that your grace and mercy are what keep me connected to your loving heart. That is the only way I can remain in you, pouring out my love and walking in your ways. Here I am again, Lord, committed to you! I remember today that whatever I do, if I am connected and rooted in you, fruit will come in time. It is so easy to get caught up in the frenzy of life and forget that you are the source of all life. Today, I center my mind around the reality of your goodness, and I remember that being connected to you is enough to produce righteous fruit. I don't need to conjure up anything when I have you for real. I love you God and bring me closer to you daily. The world is in trouble and you oh God is what the world needs.

Amen

DAY 48

Just a few words reminding us of His grace. So much grace from His fullness we all have received, grace upon grace. There are moments, when we survived things, that were meant to take us out. Understanding that it was by His grace; "We Yet Stand "(Romans 5:2 NIV)! Today I am reminded that where I have seen lack, you see an opportunity -a place that is ready to receive kindness out of the abundance of your character and kingdom. It makes no difference to you if my need is spiritual, physical, or emotional. You have more than enough to fill every dry and arid place and make it new. You make it into a place of growth and beauty. I invite you into these hard places and spaces in my life. Don't hold back God. You have access to all of it.

Grace Be to You All, My Gospel Comrades!

Amen

DAY 49

Being reminded that we have hope and a future (Jeremiah 29:11 KJV). Today we choose to be liberated through God's word and His unconditional love. Chasing down every dream and blessing that fulfill our lives through God. God's word is spoken of in Proverbs 4:22 KJV as being medicine to all our flesh. It is the most powerful medicine available today, and it can heal your body without side effects. In this prophetic year of 2022, your focus will be geared toward everything that involves God's plans for your future! That also ties your family and loved ones in with your blessings because of the enlargement of your territories! Take your place in God by force. Eliminating every thought and hindrance that tries to separate you from your destiny.

I Declare and Decree That "Defeat" Is Your Enemy And "Winning" Is All You Do! You And Your House Are Both Declared Victorious!

Amen

DAY 50

I feel a major move of God in this hour!

It is in vain that you rise early and go late to rest, eating the bread of anxious toil: for he gives to his beloved sleep (Psalm 127:2 NIV). Those that are successful lose sleep. Hard work pays off and that's why we look to the hills which come to my help (Psalm 121:1-2 NIV). You are the best teacher I could ever have; I depend on you. Keep me in my lane when I would rather jump into someone else's. Give me all the wisdom and discernment I need to keep my eyes fixed on the end goal not on the challenge of the present terrain. I trust you God. All this is for you. And I dare not fully give you the glory. You can have all of it because it belongs to you, and I love releasing what's already yours. More of You and Less of Me!

Amen

DAY 51

I believe that we are in the hour where anything you ask God for is about to be released upon your house. Get ready because God has enlarged your territory for greatness. Double is about to hit your house! And so it was, when they had crossed over, that Elijah said to Elisha, "Ask what I may do for you, before I am taken away from you?" Elisha said, "Please let a double portion of your spirit be upon me" (2 Kings 2:9 KJV). What did Elisha ask for? Elisha said, please let a double portion of your spirit be upon me. Elisha asked for a big thing – a double portion of the mighty spirit of Elijah. Elisha saw how greatly the Spirit of God worked through Elijah, and he wanted the same for himself. God is about to give it unto you; good measure, pressed down, and shaken together, and running over, where you won't have room to receive it all! You've waited and believed in God for years. Well, get ready because it's here and remember that God wants you to have it, IN JESUS NAME! Whew!

Amen

DAY 52

It's time to tackle everything that tries to attack your vision and purpose! In so many ways we are separated from each other by walls we have built, walls of misunderstanding and fear, walls of hatred and injustice, walls of self-centered judgmental attitudes, and walls built on the foundation of sin. Jesus Christ died to demolish the walls that separate us from one another (Ephesians 2:11-22KJV). Shouldn't we be committed to tearing down the walls that keep us apart today? Well today it's time for everyone to thrive! The Bible declares: That I have prayed for thee, that thy faith fails not: and when thou art converted, strengthen thy brethren (Luke22:32 KJV). Let us pray. Help us Lord, not to erect new walls that keep others from your grace. Free us from a judgmental and haughty attitude. In all of my relationships, may I demonstrate your grace and mercy, living sacrificially helping others as you did when You died for us.

Amen

DAY 53

Give thanks in all circumstances. for this is the will of God in Christ Jesus for you (1 THESSALONIANS 5:18 ESV). Good God, today I come to you with an open heart and intentions set on you. Where I would normally react in negativity to unexpected challenges in my day, help me to turn it into gratitude. I know that You can use anything to better me, and I want to be more like You. When testing comes, may I learn to creatively turn it into an opportunity to find something to be thankful for. There is no circumstance that does not have potential to be turned into a place of praise. May I become a master praise-spinner, seeing the openings for your love to shine through. As I practice the habit of gratitude, I know that it will come easier. I will more quickly see the areas that whisper your mercy. However big or small, every situation can be turned on its head in my thought-life by finding a path of appreciation. Jesus, may You be glorified in my mind.

Amen

DAY 54

Today, I would like to challenge you to let this day be a day of thanksgiving. No matter what you might be facing, the good news is this, you woke up. He's given us today. And if we're still here, living and breathing, may our every breath bring honor to Him. Be assured my friend, you never fight the battles alone. Stay strong! Choose joy! Choose to be grateful for it "all," for He is building greatness! He's working things out for our good. He hears our prayers, He sees all, and knows all. He has purpose for our pain and brings hope for our tomorrow. "I will praise God's name in song and glorify him with thanksgiving" (Psalm 69:30 KJV). Be encouraged to celebrate each moment and milestone in life knowing that it was God that brought you this far.

Amen

DAY 55

Get up because the love of God won't keep you waiting. "For God so loved the world, that he gave his only Son, that whoever believes in Him should not perish but have eternal life" John 3:16KJV. The love of God will guide you, establish you, empower you, and fully delight you. His love will free you, compel you, and sustain you. His love for you is eternal, real, and right now. All you need to do is simply open your heart to Him and set aside a little time right now to receive His amazing gift of love. "Know, in all these things we are more than conquerors through Him who loved us. For I am sure that neither death nor life, nor angels nor rulers, nor things present nor things to come, nor powers, nor height nor depth, nor anything else in all creation, will be able to separate us from the love of God in Christ Jesus our Lord" (Romans 8:37-39KJV). God's love is eternal and always trust for sure; that the love he has for you is undying. Go ahead and make this day great knowing that the great one (God) walk with you!

Amen

DAY 56

You are more than ready to face today with confirmed confidence: knowing that it will be both great and amazing. God has placed in you the hidden recipe to always get up after any and every fall. You are forever victorious! God never promised us things will be easy, but He always equips us for the battles. After David tries on the King's armor, he wisely realizes he must be who God has made him to be and use what God has given him to use (Deuteronomy 20:4 NKJV). He was not a trained soldier, but a shepherd. He wasn't skilled in sword fighting, but he was lethal with a sling and a stone. David defeated Goliath by trusting in the Lord and being true to who he was. Whatever giants you're facing today, know that, just like David, God has already given you everything you need to win. Remember, God is our refuge and strength, present help in days of trouble, He is our shield, He is our protector, He is the good shepherd, when we totally depend on His deliverance; He will fight the battle for us and give us the victory.

Now Go Ahead and Make This Day Great!

Amen

DAY 57

Today is a new day to bring yourself in alignment with your future and not your past. Remember: Let this mind be in you, which is also in Christ Jesus: (Philippians 2:5 NKJV) and know that changing your life was the best decision you could have ever made. Many people say they are Christians but fail to live according to the Bible. Yet, they wonder why they do not have the joy, peace, love, and power that God promises. How different their lives would be if they truly focused on the Word and made it their foundation. This year, make a commitment to read and study the Bible every day. In your life, make sure that you begin every day with the Word. As you have difficult decisions to make, fill your mind with the Word. Let it provide your standards. The Word will give you wisdom, and will help shape your mind and heart, and give you discernment and a victorious lifestyle. And it will prepare you to receive more of God's blessings, today, and every day.

Amen

DAY 58

I want to challenge you not to worry because whatever you give to God: He will take care of it!

"Therefore, do not worry about tomorrow, for tomorrow will worry about itself. Each day has enough trouble of its own" (Matthew 6:34 NIV). Are you worrying about what will happen tomorrow or in the future? Is something weighing down your heart so much that it is difficult to find joy in living? Life can bring many trials, sickness, pain, and sorrow, but Jesus knew you would have trials and provided words of encouragement in the Bible to help you make it through those times of doubt and worry. When you are hit by life's trials, please know that if you call upon Jesus to help you, he will be there for you. In the gospels you will find that Jesus was full of compassion and was constantly healing those who were sick. He cares about you and your needs. He hears your prayers. He knows your thoughts, worries, and fears. He alone can calm your spirit. It is very necessary that you surrender what is troubling you into the hands of Christ. If you cannot control the situation, then you must give it to Christ and trust Him to take care of it. Remember, thou wilt keep him in perfect peace, whose mind is stayed on thee: because he trusted in thee (Isaiah 26:3 NKJV). God got you! Keep living because your best days are ahead of you!

Amen

DAY 59

In Christ, we will certainly see joyful times, just as anyone does. But what truly sets us apart as followers of Jesus is that we can find victory in the most difficult trials. James knew that type of struggle very well, and yet he could honestly say: "Consider it pure joy, my brothers, whenever you face trials of many kinds, because you know that the testing of your faith develops perseverance. Perseverance must finish its work so that you may be mature and complete, not lacking anything" (James 1:2–4 NKJV). Christ gives us the strength to not only endure the tough times, but also to grow during them. As a believer: you must understand that no matter what afflictions you may face, God will deliver you out of them all (Psalm 34:19 NKJV).

Amen

DAY 60

Remember that your mouth is a weapon and today you will use it to build up others and not tear them down! Every word we speak matters. Our words can pour love, joy, comfort, and clarity into the lives of the people around us. Or they can rip those same people to the core of their being. It's up to us to carefully consider the words we speak. "Death and life are in the power of the tongue" (Proverbs 18:21 NKJV). The impact our words have on others cannot be overstated. One small comment or remark can make the difference between building a relationship up or tearing it down. A kind, positive or encouraging word at the right time can truly be life changing. We have the power to either encourage or destroy others with our speech. It's time to declare and decree! Not only will you prosper but everything that's attached to you will advance also. Having God's Holy Spirit to lead us and guide us; helps our journey in life much easier. Let's Go! Our journey will be greater than when we first started!

Amen

DAY 61

Let's open with a prayer and end with purpose!

Dear God, You are a God of overcoming and freedom. Thank you that You love us too much to leave us the way we are. You have designed us to be victorious. Help us to recognize the dangers and believe in Your power to overcome. In Jesus' name! If we give in, if we reflect the same attitudes and actions as the world, we have succumbed to the world and to the wiles of the devil. We have lost our testimony and all power to witness. But if our dependence is on the life of the Son of God, His life is in us, and then, "This is the victory that has overcome the world, even our faith" (1 John 5:4 NKJV). Being more than a conqueror means whatever the enemy intended to use to take you out — whatever was meant to destroy you — did not in fact destroy you, and it's now being used for God's glory. "I have told you these things, so that in Me you may have peace. In this world you will have trouble. But take heart! I have overcome the world" (John 16:33 NIV). Now go ahead and be great! Knowing that God did it for you!

Amen

DAY 62

God doesn't want us living in error; He wants to turn our weakness into strength, our faults into attributes, our falseness into truth, our confusion into clarity, and our messes into messages. Although I would prefer correction from the comforting voice of someone who truly cares for me, some of the best advice I ever received came seasoned with a little spite and rancor. God used a talking donkey to give His message to Balaam and He will use both sensitive and firm believers and unbelievers to send His correction to us. Just because the truth sometimes hurt doesn't mean it isn't true. My brethren: don't reject the Lord's discipline, and don't be upset when he corrects you. For the Lord corrects those he loves, just as a father corrects a child in whom he delights [Proverbs 3:11-12 (NLT)]. When we start to change our lives; always be attentive to what's right. Because the thing that you may not agree with, could be the one thing that is holding you back from being the greatest, you can be. Hang in there and strive to be the best!

Amen

DAY 63

Today's a new day, a chance for a new start. Consider it to be new opportunity to love, give, and be all that you can be in God. Your mind is one of the most powerful and creative tools that God has given you to shape your reality, influence your life and make you more than a conqueror. Romans 8:37-39 NKJV tells us that "in all things, we are more than conquerors through him who loved us. For I am convinced that neither death nor life, neither angels nor demons, neither the present nor the future, nor any powers, neither height nor depth, nor anything else in creation, will be able to separate us from the love of God that is in Jesus our Lord." This means that with God on your side; You can never be defeated. Everything you are about to walk into is far greater than everything you left behind! Get excited because this next phase of your life will be worth every moment!

Amen

DAY 64

You may be indeed doing all that you know how to do and yet there seem to be challenges and struggles that you've gone through, and you are asking in your mind, "when will I see the breakthrough"? Let me help you…right now! You must speak by faith and decide when to get up! There are times when believers think that persecutions and trials only come because of disobedience to God and that if you do what's right you won't ever have to go through trials. Yet this is not the case. Jesus said in John 16:33 NKJV, "These things I have spoken unto you, that in me ye might have peace. In the world ye shall have tribulation: But be of good cheer: I have overcome the world".

You Are Stronger Than You Could Ever Imagine!

"My Grace is sufficient for thee: for my strength is made perfect in weakness" (2 Corinthians 12:9 NKJV).

Amen

DAY 65

Let's dive in quickly with today's word! Let's go!

Therefore, my beloved brethren, be ye steadfast, unmovable, always abounding in the work of the Lord, forasmuch as ye know that your labor is not in vain in the Lord" (1 Corinthians 15:58 NKJV). The more we know about God, the better equipped we are to serve God as we serve others. It is how we grow spiritually and how we develop a deep root system. You cannot be immovable if you are planted deeply in the Word of God. You need a deep-rooted system to be immovable. I want to remind you today; that you are doing good just to remain sane! Stay planted, because it's God that's holding you up! The good news is that even if no one mentions the good work you're doing, God sees it. He never slumbers nor sleeps. He is ever-present. There is no good thing you've done in his name that he hasn't taken note of. He loves you just that much! And there is nothing you can do about it!

Amen

DAY 66

Let's not forget to make a declaration today! There is nothing in this earth realm that can stop you but yourself. God has given you the keys to unlock your breakthrough. Go ahead and allow your mouth to be a weapon of warfare that enables you to pull your blessings down. Matthew 18:18 NKJV, "Truly I tell you, whatever you bind on earth will be bound in heaven, and whatever you loose on earth will be loosed in heaven". Everything that tried to slow you down in this season has been dismantled! News Flash! You Win! Period!

Amen

DAY 67

"Brethren, I count not myself to have apprehended: but this one thing I do, forgetting those things which are behind, and reaching forth unto those things which are before" (Philippians 3:13 NKJV).

When we let go and let God, we are submitting fully to Him. We are letting go of whatever we've been trying to do on our own, so God can do what only He can do. Surrendering to God is literally giving up. It is telling God that we are not big enough to deal with our worries, and He must take over. When we finally let go, we give God room to wield his mighty arm in our lives. When our hands are weak and tired, God's hands are strong and powerful. Do not take yesterday's mistakes into the clean slate of today. Mentally shave off every single worry, doubt, fear, mistake, and anxiety from your mind each morning. Go ahead and let go; so, this day can be the best one, you've had in a long time!

Amen

DAY 68

Let's dive in with scripture! Get up and put the enemy under your feet where he belongs! You have been given authority. That authority does not rest in your strength, power, or abilities. That authority is in you because you are in a relationship with Jesus. Jesus came and spoke to them, saying, "All authority has been given to me in heaven and on earth and go, I am with you always, even to the end of the age" (Matthew 28:18 NKJV). Until Jesus Christ returns to the earth, we are bearers of his authority. Demons must submit to you and me not because of who we are, but because of who he is. Sickness must submit to you and me not because of whom we are, but because of the authority of Jesus. The name of Jesus is like a badge. It carries authority. When you use his name, you are using a name that is higher than any other name. He has given you complete authority! I know it, you know it, and the devil knows it!

YOU ARE POWERFUL AND JESUS DID IT!

Amen

DAY 69

Let's get it started by dropping a scripture! "And you shall receive power when the Holy Ghost has come upon you; and you shall be my witnesses in Jerusalem and in all Judea and Samaria and to the end of the earth"(Acts 1:8 NIV). The power is essential for the challenges of an ever-expanding witness to Christ. In other words, there is an extraordinary power available to believers, a power that can accomplish far more than we ordinarily think or imagine. It comes by the Spirit. It accords with the riches of God's glory. We should ask God for the power of His Spirit. And sometimes we should do this with fasting. Luke 4:14 NIV says that Jesus came from his 40 days fast full of the Holy Spirit. It may be that God reserves his extraordinary power for those who long for it in extraordinary ways. When we receive His power; we choose a life of integrity so that we can move forward into the abundant life He has prepared for us.

Amen

DAY 70

Today we are going to reflect on the fact that God always comes through for his people! He loves you just that much and there's nothing you can do about it! "And God is able to bless you abundantly, so that in all things at all times, having all that you need, you will abound in every good work" (2 Corinthians 9:8 NIV). The Hebrew word for bless means to kneel. Used metaphorically here, it shows that God bends down to give us Himself and with that, all His benefits – His faithfulness, mercy, forgiveness, grace, love, comfort, joy, hope, guidance, redemption, adoption, acceptance and more. Ephesians 1:3 NIV tells us we have every spiritual blessing through Jesus. Because God is infinite, we can never reach the end of His blessing. Lord, thank you for preparing blessings for me even now. Thank you for creating me to seek you. I pray for patience in the "grace periods" of life — and a deeper longing to be transformed into your image.

Amen

DAY 71

Get up and get moving; someone needs your smile today! Don't repay evil for evil. Don't retaliate with insults when people insult you. Instead, pay them back with a blessing. That is what God has called you to do, and he will grant you, his blessing (1 Peter 3:9 NIV). "I will bless those who bless you, and whoever curses you I will curse; and all people on earth will be blessed through you "(Genesis 12:3NIV). Remember; you are too blessed to be stressed. Today choose to walk in love because God will handle what you can't! Live like it's your last day here, laugh until it hurts, love like its nobody's business because God will always have your back!

Amen

DAY 72

Trust in the Lord with all thine heart; and lean not unto thine own understanding. In all thy ways acknowledge him, and he shall direct thy paths (Proverbs 3:5-6 NIV).

Sometimes your own thoughts can get you in trouble. Even when our thoughts betray us, and we find ourselves consumed with should haves and what ifs, the amazing thing is that God knows us. He examines the thoughts and intentions of our hearts. When it comes to our overthinking, we need to rebuke and correct ourselves with the truths of what Jesus has done, what he is doing, and what he will do. Search me, O God, and know my heart! Try me and know my thoughts! (Psalm 139:23KJV)

Let's Stay Focused!

Amen

DAY 73

*"Let everything that hath breath praise the
LORD. Praise ye the LORD"*

(Psalms 150:6 KJV). Praise is not just clapping your hands or applauding God. It is showing respect, honor, and gratefulness, using your whole heart, mind, spirit and body despite your circumstances. Praising God should become second nature for all believers. "This shall be written for the generation to come and the people which shall be created shall praise the Lord" (Psalm 102:18 KJV). We were created to praise God, and it becomes a natural expression of your love for the Father when you spend time in the Word and meditate on his goodness. Always remember to thank Him while you're in the midst of your circumstances. Doing this shows that you trust Him to bring you all the way out!

Amen

DAY 74

Whatever you do, don't get tired of being positive! It's your ticket for elevation! You need to recognize that Satan is using the evil and negative things of this world to discourage you, even if they are not your personal problems. You can get discouraged watching politics, reading the newspaper, and listening to the news. If you don't resist this, it will cause you to be discouraged and dismayed, and worst of all, your love for God will grow cold (Matt. 24:12NLT). The Bible says in Isaiah 26:3 NKJV that the Lord will keep him in perfect peace, whose mind is stayed upon him because he trusts in him. Our peace is linked directly to what we think. As soon as your brain starts walking down the path of negativity, put the brakes on. As a Christian, it's time for you to fight for your thoughts, because your mind won't automatically come into agreement with God's plans.

YOU HAVE TO TAKE IT BY FORCE!

So please "Be Careful "what you think because your thoughts could run your life (Proverbs 4:23 CEV)!

Amen

DAY 75

"If you faint in the day of adversity, your strength is small ... the righteous falls seven times and rises again, but the wicked stumble in times of calamity" (Proverbs 24:10, 16 NIV).

Be relentless! If you fall, get up, as many times as necessary. Proverb says, getting back up is a characteristic of people who trust God. I love what the first chapter of James says: "Count it all joy, my brothers, when you meet trials of various kinds, for you know that the testing of your faith produces steadfastness. And let steadfastness have its full effect, that you may be perfect and complete, lacking in nothing" (James 1.2-4 NIV). Every Christian is given a periodic adversity test that reveals the current status of their faith. When that happens to you don't be resentful; be thankful. Circumstances don't make or break you. They simply reveal you. That's why sometimes you are bent, instead of broken!

I'm Running on This One!

Amen

DAY 76

Make it happen today!

Here's a scripture to prove it.

"But thou shalt remember the Lord thy God: for it is he that giveth the power to get wealth" (Deuteronomy 8:18 KJV). God gives power to become rich, wealthy, and successful, then he must not be against riches, wealth and success. He must want us to be rich, wealthy, and successful. God has been a giver from the very beginning. His original plan for man was a blessing and increase (Psalm 115:14-16 KJV). The first thing God did after He created man was bless him (Genesis 1:26 – 28 KJV). Blessed means to prosper and increase as a result of God's favor upon your life. We don't just receive spiritual blessings, but they are manifested in the natural realm as well (Ephesians 1:3 KJV). When we stop believing the lies of the enemy; that's when we become free to live the abundant, victorious, and prosperous life that was promised to us. Let no one make you feel bad for having things you've earned; because choosing God was the very thing that changed your life to begin with.

Amen

DAY 77

Make the impossible happen today! Your abundance awaits you and no Demon can stop it! "The thief comes only to steal and kill and destroy. I came that they may have life and have it abundantly" (John 10:10 KJV). The thief, Satan, comes to rob us of the life that Jesus came to give. He wants to steal away our joy, kill any sense of peace that comes with knowing Christ and destroying the secure foundation we can find in Jesus. He wants us to believe the lie that this life on earth just can't get any better than it is right now. He wants us to believe that we will always have regrets from past sins, that we can't get out of the situation we live in and that we will never be good enough. But Jesus declares that He came to give us an abundant life. That's not a life of "just getting by" or hoping things will someday get better. In Christ, we can claim that the better life starts right now. We can have complete faith in the fact that He has great plans for our lives. We can have joy, because we know He loves us more than we could ever imagine possible.

Today I challenge you...to believe in your purpose. Take the world by storm with no worries. God and His angel armies are with us and fighting for us against any foe.

Amen

DAY 78

Today, be an overcomer!

Overcome means to conquer or come out on top. When the enemy tries to make you feel defeated, it's a lie. Remember that you are more than a conqueror. The Holy Spirit will be your guide and a constant reminder. Even when you face impossible odds and huge mountains in your life, you are still an overcomer. Jesus said, "In this world you will have trouble. But take heart. I have overcome the world" (John 16:33 KJV). No matter what life throws at you; you are powerful and chosen. Exercise your right to live by overcoming your personal attacks.

Let's end with a prayer.

Dear Lord,

Even when it feels hard sometimes, I know you are there with me. I also know that you work all things for my good. Help me today to focus on your goodness and faithfulness as I make my way through. With this gift called life. I too shall win!

Amen

DAY 79

I'm kicking off today's word with a burial!

Jesus said unto him, "Let the dead bury the dead" (Luke 9:60 KJV). We are killing everything that's trying to hinder your future. Pull out the shovel because it's time to say good-bye to your past. Sometimes there are things we don't want to let go of because we think we may miss out if we do. Remember the man in the Bible was potentially worried about his inheritance. Are you holding onto things that you are giving more importance or priority than you should? If there are dead things in your life let them go. They may seem important, but they are keeping you from experiencing all of God's best. Jesus has great things in store for your life. Reaching and obtaining those things require you to make following His will for your life your top priority and your greatest urgency. It's a place you and I must get to and stay in. There are always going to be things that want to compete with this priority and urgency. Despite those things let's keep following Jesus and let the dead bury their own dead.

Let's pray:

Lord,

Thank you for the truth that your grace is sufficient and help me to truly apply this in my life from this day forward.

Amen

DAY 80

No more tears because victory awaits you! So, let's kick off today with scripture! "Weeping may endure for a night, but joy cometh in the morning" (Psalm 30:5 KJV). No night lasts forever. The sun will always rise, and with the dawn comes the blessing and favor of the Father, who is hard at work to bless, strengthen, and deliver His children. David had seen this time and time again. Life may not be perfect, comfortable, or free of pain and struggle, not even for the most faithful servant of God. But during our pain, uncertainty, and fear, God is always with us and working for us. "Do not fear, for God has redeemed you; He has summoned you by name. You are Mine.... When you pass through the waters, I will be with you; and when you pass through the rivers, they will not sweep over you. When you walk through the fire, you will not be burned; the flames will not set you ablaze" (Isaiah 43:1-2 NKJV).

Get up and make this day great! For your darkest hours are officially over!

Amen

DAY 81

Let's get started with scripture, "Death and life are in the power of the tongue: and they that love it shall eat the fruit thereof" (Proverbs 18:21 KJV). It's time to speak some things into existence. When the Holy Spirit first falls on the disciples, he appears as a tongue of fire that rests on each of them. In that moment, they are granted power, authority, and special giftings that they use to spread the message of Jesus. While Pentecost was an extraordinary circumstance, anyone who comes by faith in Jesus is baptized in the Holy Spirit, and they receive spiritual gifts (1 Corinthians 12:4 KJV). These gifts are meant to be used to serve the mission of Jesus through the church. The Holy Spirit is also the one who empowers life transformation. The apostle Paul tells us that if we walk with the Spirit, then we will bear the fruit of the Spirit—namely love, joy, peace, patience, kindness, goodness, gentleness, faithfulness, and self-control (Galatians 5:22-23 KJV).

Amen

DAY 82

Let's get started with scripture! "But they who wait for the Lord shall renew their strength. they shall mount up with wings like eagles; they shall run and not be weary; they shall walk and not faint" (Isaiah 40:31 KJV). God uses seasons of waiting to prepare us for what's coming, to draw us closer to Him, and to make sure His promises are fulfilled at the proper time. So don't get tired. It's too early in the season to get weak.

"For the vision is yet for an appointed time, but at the end it shall speak, and not lie though it tarry, wait for it; because it will surely come, it will not tarry "(Habakkuk 2:3 KJV).

Let's end with a prayer:

Lord, turn my heart and my mind toward You and toward the role You have chosen for me to live out. Help me to put Your will and Your purpose ahead of my own. I humbly bow before You and ask for Your direction and guidance, as well as your courage to live out the calling; I've been given for such a time as this. Lord, help me so I can help myself, because I am determined not to miss my time.

Amen

DAY 83

Let's launch out with a fresh start releasing yesterday's failures. Let's get started. Paul said, "I'm forgetting those things which are behind me and reaching forward to those things which are ahead of me" (Philippians 3:13-14 KJV). I'm telling you now to shake yourself and let it go. The new you fight every day against old thoughts trying to hold you down.

IT'S OVER! AND YOU KNOW IT!

We must let go of the familiar and open our minds to possibilities of who we are supposed to be that may make no sense to anyone, just as walking through the Red Sea made no sense until it was done. This is exactly how God's dream happens.

Let Us Pray:

Lord, We break free from old rules, old ways, and old habits to become this person who has been sleeping inside. We set ourselves free from the emotional stagnation keeps us from living God's dream this day.

Today we strive to be bigger and better. Killing out all distractions as we race to the finish line to complete

WHAT GOD STARTED IN US!

Amen

DAY 84

Kicking off today's affirmations with a powerful scripture. Reminding you that when painful thoughts invade your peace, "Put the word on the enemy ". Demonstrate your victory. For the word of God is quick, and powerful, and sharper than any two-edged sword, piercing even to the dividing asunder of soul and spirit, and of the joints and marrow, and is a discerner of the thoughts and intents of the heart (Hebrews 4:12 KJV). The word of God is active. The Greek word is (energies) from which we get our word energy. It is powerful, dynamic, full of energy. It does things no human being can possibly do. It touches where nothing else can touch and brings life. It is energizing. It is the power of God. It is the most powerful weapon in the universe. And no devil or demon can stop it, once it's activated in your life!

Lord,

We thank you for the living, powerful word of God. I pray that whatever it takes, your Holy Spirit would continue to convict, convert, comfort, and conform many into the image of the lovely Lord Jesus, so that they become the person you want them to be.

Amen

DAY 85

There are times in your life when your breakthrough seems so far away.

BUT IT'S IN REACHING DISTANCE!

God never said that trouble won't hit you. He said trouble won't hold you. I'm running on this nugget! You see, sometimes, God must allow things to fall apart so He can put them back together his way. He wants more for you. So don't fret if things aren't panning out the way you had hoped they would. This is just a divine setup. God is preparing you for an awesome breakthrough. He's connecting you with some new people, taking you to some new places and showing you some new things. He's reshaping your perspective and realigning your priorities, in order to equip you to handle what he already has waiting for you. Remember this:

"For the weapons of our warfare are not carnal, but mighty through God to the pulling down of strong holds; Casting down imaginations, and every high thing that exalted itself against the knowledge of God and bringing into captivity every thought to the obedience of Christ" (2 Corinthians 10:4-5 KJV).

YOUR TIME IS NOW!

Amen

DAY 86

Let's get started with a powerful reminder!

You can do all things through Christ that strengthens you. "Now unto him that is able to do exceedingly abundantly above all that we ask or think, according to the power that worketh in us," (Ephesians 3:20 KJV) The Father said to Jesus, through the prophetic voice of David, "

The LORD says to my Lord: "Sit at my right hand, until I make your enemies your footstool" (Ps. 110:1 ESV). In other words, Jesus is at God's right hand, waiting for the Father to subdue his enemies under his feet. The right hand of the Father is a place of accomplishment after Jesus had finished what he had to do. He died, resurrected, ascended, and now sits at the right hand of the Father. Jesus is waiting for the Father to complete his work and fulfill his purpose through the believers. When we realize our position in Christ, it makes a tremendous difference in our lives, and we will no longer feel defeated.

Amen

DAY 87

Get up and move out! It's the perfect time to
reflect on your dreams and your purpose!

Whatever Satan has said, IT'S A LIE! Your future awaits you and has already been determined! Satan wants us to believe God is done with us when we stumble and fall. But this is not the truth. Paul said that because of Christ's work in us, "we are struck down but not destroyed". We can get up and get going again in our Lord's resurrection power. Be the star you are! Launch out into the deep and call down fire! By doing so, we pray that you walk in favor, authority, power, and purpose followed by victory! "Trust in the LORD with all thine heart; And lean not unto thine own understanding. In all thy ways acknowledge him, and he shall direct thy paths" (Proverbs 3:5-6 KJV). Because winning is what you do best!

Amen

DAY 88

We are going to take back everything the devil stole from us!

The Bible Declares:

That from the days of John the Baptist until now the kingdom of heaven suffered violence, and the violent take it by force (Matthew 11:12 KJV). The devil is out to steal, kill and destroy everything that belongs to you or should belong to you (John 10:10 KJV). But you were called to resist him, use your authority and stand your ground. You were called to guard what belongs to you and reclaim whatever he has stolen. But God is a God of restoration. His will is for you to recover everything that has been stolen from you so you can live in VICTORY. When God told David to pursue, He followed it by saying this: "You shall surely overtake them and without fail recover all" (1 Samuel 30:8 KJV).

This is "Guaranteed Success"!

That word is for you today!

Now go and get it all back, starting your day with ambition and determination!

Amen

DAY 89

Let's arise, and give God Glory because it is one more day that "The Lord" has kept us! With all that's going on in the world, leaving God is the last thing that should be on anybody's mind. It's not an option. When you're hurting, in trouble, or waiting for answers in your life, you need to believe that your help has been sent out from heaven and it is on the way. God may not come early, but He won't be late. Not only will God deliver you, but He will also sustain you while you're waiting for your breakthrough. He keeps us strong while we're waiting and keeps us from going under (Isaiah 41:10 NKJV). So, no matter what your circumstances look like or what the world may say, hang in there. Because help is on the way! But those who trust in the LORD will find new strength. They will soar high on wings like eagles. They will run and not grow weary. They will walk and not faint (Isaiah 40:31 NKJV).

Amen

DAY 90

Get on the mark!

Because it's finally your turn to run!

Today, you might be on lap number seven around your "Jericho" and not even know it. Suppose they had stopped on day six, saying, this is ridiculous. I'm not feeling it. Not one stone has fallen to the ground. I don't see any progress. They would have missed the blessing (Joshua 6:1-27 KJV). There will be times when you're doing everything you know to do, and you still don't see any movement. The Israelites walked around Jericho for six days, and as far as they could tell, nothing happened. I'm sure it unnerved the people behind the wall, but as far as the walkers could tell, not one brick fell. Then suddenly after obedience, THE ENTIRE CITY FELL! You never know what God will do next. So, stay right where you are trusting God until every wall comes tumbling down! You were built for this!

Amen

PRAYERS

Lord,

According to your divine purpose and will for my life, I understand that the weapons of our warfare are not of the flesh but have divine power to destroy strongholds. Today I choose to utilize my power you have given us. I surrender to the authority that you invested through your Son in His obedience: giving us power to defeat our enemies. Today I stand. I have the assurance that I can do all things through Christ (You) which strengthens me. I am more than a conqueror.

Amen

Lord,

Today I accept the mistakes I've made. Knowing that you are just to forgive me. Lord, I surrender all; and pray with strong belief that you will use all of me. Thank you for never giving up on me, even when the hours of serving you were limited. Now I take full accountability over my life and ready for You to finish the work that You have started in me.

Amen

Heavenly Father…

The forgiver of our sins.

Thank you for always hearing and answering our prayers. We pray for stronger faith. When Jesus saw the paralytic man being lowered through on the roof, He saw the faith of the man's friends. Their faith was a belief that Jesus could do something about their situation. Give us that same faith. Please help us to come to You with all our problems and pressures, knowing that if we come to You, you can change the situation. We can do all things through Christ that strengthens us! You are the King of Ages, immortal, invisible, the only God. Giving you all the honor and glory forever and ever, through Jesus Christ, our Lord.

Amen

Dear Reader,

When life gets overwhelming, we tend to forget the blessings in our life. With life's problems knocking at your door, it can be difficult to manage things that we shouldn't forget. For example, where did you put your keys, or you may have forgotten to say thank you to someone who went above and beyond, and just completely forgot to communicate with God. Over time, we lose the gratitude and appreciation we have for the blessings in our life. That's why I wrote these heartfelt devotions of power to encourage all humanity in need of God's love. The gift of encouragement is important in our lives. Encouragement is a gift in the home, the workplace, the church—wherever we find ourselves. We can come alongside others and be there for one another. We can listen, comfort, console, affirm. It's a way of living out the command to love one another. Take time to recall the people who've been encouragers in your life. They're the ones who were there when you thought you'd never laugh again. They were the ones who listened to you, whereas others just talked. Then ask yourself, "When was the last time I encouraged someone"? It's not difficult, and the people you encourage are so blessed by it. Prayer knows no rules so just pray. Pure, unplugged, heart-tuned-in communication with your best friend is all you need. And of course; His name is Jesus! I pray that these daily devotionals will help you pay close attention to yourself so that you can grow as a person. I also pray that they will inspire you so that many be inspired through the knowledge and power you've gained generations to come.

Amen

JOURNAL

....
....
....
....
....
....
....
....
....
....
....
....
....
....
....

"You are my hiding place and my shield: I hope in Your word." Psalms 119:114 ESV

JOURNAL

"Delight yourself in the Lord, and he will give you the desires of your heart." Psalms 37:4KJV

JOURNAL

....
....
....
....
....
....
....
....
....
....
....
....
....
....
....

"Being confident of this very thing, that he which hath begun a good work in you will perform it until the day of Jesus Christ" Philippians 1:6 KJV

JOURNAL

"Be still, and know that I am God: "Psalms 46:10 KJV

JOURNAL

"The fear of the Lord is the beginning of knowledge: but fools despise wisdom and instruction." Proverbs 1:7 NIV

JOURNAL

"And above all things have fervent charity among yourselves: for charity shall cover the multitude of sins." 1 Peter 4:8 KJV

JOURNAL

....

....

....

....

....

....

....

....

....

....

....

....

....

....

"For this day is holy unto our Lord: neither be ye sorry; for the joy of the Lord is your strength." Nehemiah 8:10 KJV

JOURNAL

"You keep him in perfect peace whose mind is stayed on you, because he trusts in you" Isaiah 26:3 NKJV

JOURNAL

....
....
....
....
....
....
....
....
....
....
....
....
....
....
....
....

"But they who wait for the Lord shall renew their strength; They shall mount up with wings like eagles, they shall run and not be weary; they shall walk and not faint." Isaiah 40:31 NKJV

JOURNAL

"We put our hope in the Lord. He is our help and our shield", Psalms 33:20 KJV

JOURNAL

"For God hasn't given us a spirit of fear, but of power and of love and of a sound mind." 2Timothy 1:7 KJV

JOURNAL

"For God so loved the world that he gave his one and only Son, that whoever believes in him shall not perish but have eternal life." John 3:16 NKJV

JOURNAL

"I can do everything through Christ who gives me strength" Philippians 4:13 KJV

JOURNAL

"For the wages of sin is death, but the gift of God is eternal life in Christ Jesus our Lord." Romans 6:23 KJV

JOURNAL

....
....
....
....
....
....
....
....
....
....
....
....
....
....

"If God is for us who can be against us" Romans 8:31 KJV

JOURNAL

....
....
....
....
....
....
....
....
....
....
....
....
....
....
....

"He who dwells in the secret place of the Most High will rest in the shadow of the Almighty" Psalms 91:1 KJV

JOURNAL

"Don't be conformed to this world but be transformed by the renewing of your mind, so that you may prove what is the good, well pleasing, and perfect will of God" Romans 12:2 NIV

JOURNAL

"And all these blessings shall come on you, and overtake you, if you shall listen to the voice of the Lord your God" Deuteronomy 28:2 KJV

JOURNAL

"But ye shall receive power, after that the Holy Ghost is come upon you: and ye shall be witnesses unto me both in Jerusalem, and in all Judaea, and in Samaria, and unto the uttermost part of the earth." Acts 1:8 KJV

JOURNAL

"Behold, I give unto you power to tread on serpents and scorpions, and over all the power of the enemy: and nothing shall by any means hurt you." Luke 10:19 NIV

JOURNAL

....
....
....
....
....
....
....
....
....
....
....
....
....
....
....
....

"But seek first the kingdom of God, and his righteousness, and all these things shall be added unto you" (Matthew 6:33) KJV